QUESTIONS & ANSWERS

SWAMI VIVEKANANDA

JOLLYJOY

ABOUT TO AUTHOR

Swami Vivekananda, born Narendranath Datta on January 12, 1863, in Kolkata, India, was a key figure in introducing Hindu philosophy to the Western world. A disciple of the mystic Ramakrishna, Vivekananda played a pivotal role in the revival of Hinduism and the promotion of Vedanta.

He gained international fame at the Parliament of Religions in Chicago in 1893, where his powerful speech emphasized the unity of all religions and the importance of tolerance. His teachings focused on the idea of self-realization, the potential of every individual, and the necessity of combining spirituality with practical action for societal betterment.

Vivekananda founded the Ramakrishna Mission in 1897, promoting social service, education, and spiritual development. His writings, including "Raja Yoga" and "Karma Yoga," delve into the practical applications of yoga and the importance of selfless action.

A visionary thinker, he inspired generations with his ideas on spirituality, nationalism, and human potential, leaving a lasting legacy that continues to influence millions worldwide. Swami Vivekananda passed away on January 19, 1902, but his teachings remain relevant, advocating for the harmony of science and spirituality, and encouraging individuals to pursue their highest potential.

Questions & Answers

by Swami Vivekananda

Published by Jollyjoy Books Pvt Ltd.

JOLLYJOY
BOOKS

4771/23, Bharat Ram Road, Daryaganj,

New Delhi-110002

E-mail: Contact@jollyjoybooks.com

ISBN: 978-93-6849-648-9

Cover, Typesetting, and Book Design by JollyJoy Books

Contents

A DISCUSSION

This discussion followed the lecture on the Vedanta Philosophy delivered by the Swami at the Graduate Philosophical Society of Harvard University, U. S. A., on March 25, 1896. (Vol. I.

Q. — I should like to know something about the present activity of philosophic thought in India. To what extent are these questions discussed?

A. — As I have said, the majority of the Indian people are practically dualists, and the minority are monists. The main subject of discussion is Mâyâ and Jiva. When I came to this country, I found that the labourers were informed of the present condition of politics; but when I asked them, "What is religion, and what are the doctrines of this and that particular sect?" they said, "We do not know; we go to church." In India if I go to a peasant and ask him, "Who governs you?" he says, "I do not know; I pay my taxes." But if I ask him what is his religion, he says, "I am a dualist", and is ready to give you the details about Maya and Jiva. He cannot read or write, but he has learned all this from the monks and is very fond of discussing it. After the day's work, the peasants sit under a tree and discuss these questions.

Q. — What does orthodoxy mean with the Hindus?

A. — In modern times it simply means obeying certain caste

laws as to eating, drinking, and marriage. After that the Hindu can believe in any system he likes. There was never an organised church in India; so there was never a body of men to formulate doctrines of orthodoxy. In a general way, we say that those who believe in the Vedas are orthodox; but in reality we find that many of the dualistic sects believe more in the Purânas than in the Vedas alone.

Q. — What influence had your Hindu philosophy on the Stoic philosophy of the Greeks?

A. — It is very probable that it had some influence on it through the Alexandrians. There is some suspicion of Pythagoras' being influenced by the Sânkhya thought. Anyway, we think the Sankhya philosophy is the first attempt to harmonise the philosophy of the Vedas through reason. We find Kapila mentioned even in the Vedas: " — He who (supports through knowledge) the first-born sage Kapila."

Q. — What is the antagonism of this thought with Western science?

A. — No antagonism at all. We are in harmony with it. Our theory of evolution and of Âkâsha and Prâna is exactly what your modern philosophies have. Your belief in evolution is among our Yogis and in the Sankhya philosophy. For instance, Patanjali speaks of one species being changed into another by the infilling of nature — " "; only he differs from you in the explanation. His explanation of this evolution is spiritual. He says that just as when a farmer wants to water his field from the canals that pass near, he has only to lift up gate — " " — so each man is the Infinite already, only these bars and bolts and different circumstances shut him in; but as soon as they are removed, he rushes out and expresses himself. In the animal, the man was held in abeyance; but as soon as good circumstances came, he was manifested as man. And again, as soon as fitting circumstances came, the God in man manifested itself. So we have very little to quarrel with in the new theories. For instance, the theory of the Sankhya as to perception is very little different from modern physiology.

Q. — But your method is different?

A. — Yes. We claim that concentrating the powers of the mind is the only way to knowledge. In external science, concentration of mind is — putting it on something external; and in internal science, it is — drawing towards one's Self. We call this concentration of mind Yoga.

Q. — In the state of concentration does the truth of these principles become evident?

A.— The Yogis claim a good deal. They claim that by concentration of the mind every truth in the universe becomes evident to the mind, both external and internal truth.

Q. — What does the Advaitist think of cosmology?

A. — The Advaitist would say that all this cosmology and everything else are only in Maya, in the phenomenal world. In truth they do not exist. But as long as we are bound, we have to see these visions. Within these visions things come in a certain regular order. Beyond them there is no law and order, but freedom.

Q. — Is the Advaita antagonistic to dualism?

A. — The Upanishads not being in a systematised form, it was easy for philosophers to take up texts when they liked to form a system. The Upanishads had always to be taken, else there would be no basis. Yet we find all the different schools of thought in the Upanishads. Our solution is that the Advaita is not antagonistic to the Dvaita (dualism). We say the latter is only one of three steps. Religion always takes three steps. The first is dualism. Then man gets to a higher state, partial non-dualism. And at last he finds he is one with the universe. Therefore the three do not contradict but fulfil.

Q. — Why does Maya or ignorance exist?

A. — "Why" cannot be asked beyond the limit of causation. It can only be asked within Maya. We say we will answer the question when it is logically formulated. Before that we have no right to answer.

Q.— Does the Personal God belong to Maya?

A. — Yes; but the Personal God is the same Absolute seen through Maya. That Absolute under the control of nature is what is called the human soul; and that which is controlling nature is Ishvara, or the Personal God. If a man starts from here to see the sun, he will see at first a little sun; but as he proceeds he will see it bigger and bigger, until he reaches the real one. At each stage of his progress he was seeing apparently a different sun; yet we are sure it was the same sun he was seeing. So all these things are but visions of the Absolute, and as such they are true. Not one is a false vision, but we can only say they were lower stages.

Q. — What is the special process by which one will come to know the Absolute?

A. — We say there are two processes. One is the positive, and the other, the negative. The positive is that through which the whole universe is going — that of love. If this circle of love is increased indefinitely, we reach the one universal love. The other is the "Neti", "Neti" — "not this", "not this" — stopping every wave in the mind which tries to draw it out; and at last the mind dies, as it were, and the Real discloses Itself. We call that Samâdhi, or superconsciousness.

Q. — That would be, then, merging the subject in the object!

A. — Merging the object in the subject, not merging the subject in the object. Really this world dies, and I remain. I am the only one that remains.

Q. — Some of our philosophers in Germany have thought that the whole doctrine of Bhakti (Love for the Divine) in India was very likely the result of occidental influence.

A. — I do not take any stock in that — the assumption was ephemeral. The Bhakti of India is not like the Western Bhakti. The central idea of ours is that there is no thought of fear. It is always, love God. There is no worship through fear, but always through love, from beginning to end. In the second place, the assumption is quite unnecessary. Bhakti is spoken of in the oldest of the Upanishads, which is much older than the Christian Bible. The germs of Bhakti are even in the Samhitâ (the Vedic hymns). The word Bhakti is not a

Western word. It was suggested by the word Shraddhâ.

Q. — What is the Indian idea of the Christian faith?

A. — That it is very good. The Vedanta will take in every one. We have a peculiar idea in India. Suppose I had a child. I should not teach him any religion; I should teach him breathings — the practice of concentrating the mind, and just one line of prayer — not prayer in your sense, but simply something like this, "I meditate on Him who is the Creator of this universe: may He enlighten my mind I " That way he would be educated, and then go about hearing different philosophers and teachers. He would select one who, he thought, would suit him best; and this man would become his Guru or teacher, and he would become a Shishya or disciple. He would say to that man, "This form of philosophy which you preach is the best; so teach me." Our fundamental idea is that your doctrine cannot be mine, or mine yours. Each one must have his own way. My daughter may have one method, and my son another, and I again another. So each one has an Ishta or chosen way, and we keep it to ourselves. It is between me and my teacher, because we do not want to create a fight. It will not help any one to tell it to others, because each one will have to find his own way. So only general philosophy and general methods can be taught universally. For instance, giving a ludicrous example, it may help me to stand on one leg. It would be ludicrous to you if I said every one must do that, but it may suit me. It is quite possible for me to be a dualist and for my wife to be a monist, and so on. One of my sons may worship Christ or Buddha or Mohammed, so long as he obeys the caste laws. That is his own Ishta.

Q. — Do all Hindus believe in caste?

A. — They are forced to. They may not believe, but they have to obey.

Q. — Are these exercises in breathing and concentration universally practiced?

A. — Yes; only some practice only a little, just to satisfy the requirements of their religion. The temples in India are not like the churches here. They may all vanish tomorrow, and will not be missed. A temple is built by a man who wants to go to heaven, or to get a son, or something of that sort. So he builds a large temple and employs a few priests to hold services there. I need not go there at all, because all my worship is in the home. In every house is a special room set apart, which is called the chapel. The first duty of the child, after his initiation, is to take a bath, and then to worship; and his worship consists of this breathing and meditating and repeating of a certain name. And another thing is to hold the body straight. We believe that the mind has every power over the body to keep it healthy. After one has done this, then another comes and takes his seat, and each one does it in silence. Sometimes there are three or four in the same room, but each one may have a different method. This worship is repeated at least twice a day.

Q. — This state of oneness that you speak of, is it an ideal or something actually attained?

A. — We say it is within actuality; we say we realise that state. If it were only in talk, it would be nothing. The Vedas teach three things: this Self is first to be heard, then to be reasoned, and then to be meditated upon. When a man first hears it, he must reason on it, so that he does not believe it ignorantly, but knowingly; and after reasoning what it is, he must meditate upon it, and then realise it. And that is religion. Belief is no part of religion. We say religion is a superconscious state.

Q. — If you ever reach that state of superconsciousness, can you ever tell about it?

A. — No; but we know it by its fruits. An idiot, when he goes to sleep, comes out of sleep an idiot or even worse. But another man goes into the state of meditation, and when he comes out he is a philosopher, a sage, a great man. That shows the difference between these two states.

Q. — I should like to ask, in continuation of Professor —'s question, whether you know of any people who have made any study of the principles of self-hypnotism, which they undoubtedly practiced to a great extent in ancient India, and what has been recently stated and practiced in that thing. Of course you do not have it so much in modern India.

A. — What you call hypnotism in the West is only a part of the real thing. The Hindus call it self-hypnotisation. They say you are hypnotised already, and that you should get out of it and de-hypnotise yourself. "There the sun cannot illume, nor the moon, nor the stars; the flash of lightning cannot illume that; what to speak of this mortal fire! That shining, everything else shines" (Katha Upanishad, II ii. 15). That is not hypnotisation, but de-hypnotisation. We say that every other religion that preaches these things as real is practicing a form of hypnotism. It is the Advaitist alone that does not care to be hypnotised. His is the only system that more or less understands that hypnotism comes with every form of dualism. But the Advaitist says, throw away even the Vedas, throw away even the Personal God, throw away even the universe, throw away even your own body and mind, and let nothing remain, in order to get rid of hypnotism perfectly. "From where the mind comes back with speech, being unable to reach, knowing the Bliss of Brahman, no more is fear." That is de-hypnotisation. "I have neither vice nor virtue, nor misery nor happiness; I care neither for the Vedas nor sacrifices nor ceremonies; I am neither food nor eating nor eater, for I am Existence Absolute, Knowledge Absolute, Bliss Absolute; I am He, I am He." We know all about hypnotism. We have a psychology which the West is just beginning to know, but not yet adequately, I am sorry to say.

Q. — What do you call the astral body?

A. — The astral body is what we call the Linga Sharira. When this body dies, how can it come to take another body? Force cannot remain without matter. So a little part of the fine matter remains, through which the internal organs make another body — for each one is making his own body; it is the mind that makes the body. If I become a sage, my brain gets changed into a sage's brain; and the Yogis say that even in this life a Yogi can change his body into a god-body. The Yogis show many wonderful things. One ounce of practice is worth a thousand pounds of theory. So I have no right to say that because I have not seen this or that thing done, it is false. Their books say that with practice you can get all sorts of results that are most wonderful. Small results can be obtained in a short time by regular practice, so that one may know that there is no humbug about it, no charlatanism. And these Yogis explain the very wonderful things mentioned in all scriptures in a scientific way. The question is, how these records of miracles entered into every nation. The man, who says that they are all false and need no explanation, is not rational. You have no right to deny them until you can prove them false. You must prove that they are without any foundation, and only then have you the right to stand up and deny them. But you have not done that. On the other hand, the Yogis say they are not miracles, and they claim that they can do them even today. Many wonderful things are done in India today. But none of them are done by miracles. There are many books on the subject. Again, if nothing else has been done in that line except a scientific approach towards psychology, that credit must be given to the Yogis.

Q. — Can you say in the concrete what the manifestations are which the Yogi can show?

A. — The Yogi wants no faith or belief in his science but that which is given to any other science, just enough gentlemanly faith to come and make the experiment. The ideal of the Yogi is tremendous. I have seen the lower things that can be done by the power of the mind, and therefore, I have no right to disbelieve that the highest things can be done. The ideal of the Yogi is eternal peace and love through omniscience and omnipotence. I know a Yogi who was bitten by a cobra, and who fell down on the ground. In the evening he revived again, and when asked what happened, he said: "A messenger came from my Beloved." All hatred and anger and jealousy have been burnt out of this man. Nothing can make him react; he is infinite love all the time, and he is omnipotent in his power of love. That is the real Yogi. And this manifesting different things is accidental on the way. That is not what he wants to attain. The Yogi says, every man is a slave except the Yogi. He is a slave of food, to air, to his wife, to his children, to a dollar, slave to a nation, slave to name and fame, and to a thousand things in this world. The man who is not controlled by any one of these bandages is alone a real man, a real Yogi. "They have conquered relative existence in this life who are firm-fixed in sameness. God is pure and the same to all.

Therefore such are said to be living in God" (Gita, V. 19).

Q. — Do the Yogis attach any importance to caste?

A. — No; caste is only the training school for undeveloped minds.

Q. — Is there no connection between this idea of super-consciousness and the heat of India?

A. — I do not think so; because all this philosophy was thought out fifteen thousand feet above the level of the sea, among the Himalayas, in an almost Arctic temperature.

Q. — Is it practicable to attain success in a cold climate?

A. — It is practicable, and the only thing that is practicable in this world. We say you are a born Vedantist, each one of you. You are declaring your oneness with everything each moment you live. Every time that your heart goes out towards the world, you are a true Vedantist, only you do not know it. You are moral without knowing why; and the Vedanta is the philosophy which analysed and taught man to be moral consciously. It is the essence of all religions.

Q. — Should you say that there is an unsocial principle in our Western people, which makes us so pluralistic, and that Eastern people are more sympathetic than we are?

A. — I think the Western people are more cruel, and the Eastern people have more mercy towards all beings. But that is simply because your civilisation is very much more recent. It takes time to make a thing come under the influence of mercy. You have a great deal of power, and the power of control of the mind has especially been very little practiced. It will take time to make you gentle and good. This feeling tingles in every drop of blood in India. If I go to the villages to teach the people politics, they will not understand; but if I go to teach them Vedanta, they will say, "Now, Swami, you are all right". That Vairâgya, non-attachment, is everywhere in India, even today. We are very much degenerated now; but kings will give up their thrones and go about the country without anything.

In some places the common village-girl with her spinning-wheel says, "Do not talk to me of dualism; my spinning-wheel says 'Soham, Soham' — 'I am He, I am He.'" Go and talk to these people, and ask them why it is that they speak so and yet kneel before that stone. They will say that with you religion means dogma, but with them realisation. "I will be a Vedantist", one of them will say, "only when all this has vanished, and I have seen the reality. Until then there is no difference between me and the ignorant. So I am using these stones and am going to temples, and so on, to come to realisation. I have heard, but I want to see and realise." "Different methods of speech, different manners of explaining the meaning of the scriptures — these are only for the enjoyment of the learned, not for freedom" (Shankara). It is realisation which leads us to that freedom.

Q. — Is this spiritual freedom among the people consistent with attention to caste?

A. — Certainly not. They say there should be no caste. Even those who are in caste say it is not a very perfect institution. But they say, when you find us another and a better one, we will give it up. They say, what will you give us instead? Where is there no caste? In your nation you are struggling all the time to make a caste. As soon as a man gets a bag of dollars, he says, "I am one of the Four Hundred." We alone have succeeded in making a permanent caste. Other nations are struggling and do not succeed. We have superstitions and evils enough. Would taking the superstitions and evils from your country mend matters? It is owing to caste that three hundred millions of people can find a piece of bread to eat yet. It is an imperfect institution, no doubt. But if it had not been for caste, you would have had no Sanskrit books to study. This caste made walls, around which all sorts of invasions rolled and surged, but found it impossible to break through. That necessity has not gone yet; so caste remains. The caste we have now is not that of seven hundred years ago. Every blow has riveted it. Do you realise that India is the only country that never went outside of itself to conquer? The great emperor Asoka insisted that none of his descendants should go to conquer. If people want to send us teachers, let them help, but not injure. Why should all these people come to conquer the Hindus?

Did they do any injury to any nation? What little good they could do, they did for the world. They taught it science, philosophy, religion, and civilised the savage hordes of the earth. And this is the return — only murder and tyranny, and calling them heathen rascals. Look at the books written on India by Western people and at the stories of many travellers who go there; in retaliation for what injuries are these hurled at them?

Q. — What is the Vedantic idea of civilisation?

A. — You are philosophers, and you do not think that a bag of gold makes the difference between man and man. What is the value of all these machines and sciences? They have only one result: they spread knowledge. You have not solved the problem of want, but only made it keener. Machines do not solve the poverty question; they simply make men struggle the more. Competition gets keener. What value has nature in itself? Why do you go and build a monument to a man who sends electricity through a wire? Does not nature do that millions of times over? Is not everything already existing in nature? What is the value of your getting it? It is already there. The only value is that it makes this development. This universe is simply a gymnasium in which the soul is taking exercise; and after these exercises we become gods. So the value of everything is to be decided by how far it is a manifestation of God. Civilisation is the manifestation of that divinity in man.

Q. — Have the Buddhists any caste laws?

A. — The Buddhists never had much caste, and there are very few Buddhists in India. Buddha was a social reformer. Yet in Buddhistic countries I find that there have been strong attempts to manufacture caste, only they have failed. The Buddhists' caste is practically nothing, but they take pride in it in their own minds.

Buddha was one of the Sannyâsins of the Vedanta. He started a new sect, just as others are started even today. The ideas which now are called Buddhism were not his. They were much more ancient. He was a great man who gave the ideas power. The unique element in Buddhism was its social element. Brahmins and Kshatriyas have always been our teachers, and most of the Upanishads were written by Kshatriyas, while the ritualistic portions of the Vedas came from the Brahmins. Most of our great teachers throughout India have been Kshatriyas, and were always universal in their teachings; whilst the Brahmana prophets with two exceptions were very exclusive. Râma, Krishna, and Buddha — worshipped as Incarnations of God — were Kshatriyas.

Q. — Are sects, ceremonies, and scriptures helps to realisation?

A. — When a man realises, he gives up everything. The various sects and ceremonies and books, so far as they are the means of arriving at that point, are all right. But when they fail in that, we must change them. "The knowing one must not despise the condition of those who are ignorant, nor should the knowing one destroy the faith; of the ignorant in their own particular method, but by proper action lead them and show them the path to comes to where he stands" (Gita, III. 26).

Q. — How does the Vedanta explain individuality and ethics?

A. — The real individual is the Absolute; this personalisation is through Maya. It is only apparent; in reality it is always the Absolute. In reality there is one, but ins Maya it is appearing as many. In Maya there is this variation. Yet even in this Maya there is always the tendency to, get back to the One, as expressed in all ethics and all morality of every nation, because it is the constitutional necessity of the soul. It is finding its oneness; and this struggle to find this oneness is what we call ethics and morality. Therefore we must always practice them.

Q. — Is not the greater part of ethics taken up with the relation between individuals?

A. — That is all it is. The Absolute does not come within Maya.

Q. — You say the individual is the Absolute, and I was going to ask you whether the individual has knowledge.

A. — The state of manifestation is individuality, and the light in that state is what we call knowledge. To use, therefore, this term knowledge for the light of the Absolute is not precise, as the absolute state transcends relative knowledge.

Q. — Does it include it?

A. — Yes, in this sense. Just as a piece of gold can be changed into all sorts of coins, so with this. The state can be broken up into all sorts of knowledge. It is the state of superconsciousness, and includes both consciousness and unconsciousnes. The man who attains that state has all that we call knowledge. When he wants to realise that consciousness of knowledge, he has to go a step lower. Knowledge is a lower state; it is only in Maya that we can have knowledge.

At the Twentieth Century Club of Boston, U. S. A.

Q. — Did Vedanta exert any influence over Mohammedanism?

A. — This Vedantic spirit of religious liberality has very much affected Mohammedanism. Mohammedanism in India is quite a different thing from that in any other country. It is only when Mohammedans come from other countries and preach to their co-religionists in India about living with men who are not of their faith that a Mohammedan mob is aroused and fights.

Q. — Does Vedanta recognise caste?

A. — The caste system is opposed to the religion of the Vedanta. Caste is a social custom, and all our great preachers have tried to break it down. From Buddhism downwards, every sect has preached against caste, and every time it has only riveted the chains. Caste is simply the outgrowth of the political institutions of India; it is a hereditary trade guild. Trade competition with Europe has broken caste more than any teaching.

Q. — What is the peculiarity of the Vedas?

A. — One peculiarity of the Vedas is that they are the only

scriptures that again and again declare that you must go beyond them. The Vedas say that they were written just for the child mind; and when you have grown, you must go beyond them.

Q. — Do you hold the individual soul to be eternally real?

A. — The individual soul consists of a man's thoughts, and they are changing every moment. Therefore, it cannot be eternally real. It is real only in the phenomenal. The individual consists of memory and thought, how can that be real?

Q. — Why did Buddhism as a religion decline in India?

A. — Buddhism did not really decline in India; it was only a gigantic social movement. Before Buddha great numbers of animals were killed for sacrifice and other reasons, and people drank wine and ate meat in large quantities. Since Buddha's teaching drunkenness has almost disappeared, and the killing of animals has almost gone.

At the Brooklyn Ethical Society, Brooklyn, U. S. A.

Q. — How can you reconcile your optimistic views with the existence of evil, with the universal prevalence of sorrow and pain?

A. — I can only answer the question if the existence of evil be first proved; but this the Vedantic religion does not admit. Eternal pain unmixed with pleasure would be a positive evil; but temporal pain and sorrow, if they have contributed an element of tenderness and nobility tending towards eternal bliss, are not evils: on the contrary, they may be supreme good. We cannot assert that anything is evil until we have traced its sequence into the realm of eternity. Devil worship is not a part of the Hindu religion. The human race is in process of development; all have not reached the same altitude. Therefore some are nobler and purer in their earthly lives than others. Every one has an opportunity within the limits of the sphere of his present development of making himself better. We cannot unmake ourselves; we cannot destroy or impair the vital force within us, but we have the freedom to give it different directions.

Q. — Is not the reality of cosmic matter simply the imagining of our own minds?

A. — In my opinion the external world is certainly an entity and has an existence outside of our mental conceptions. All creation is moving onwards and upwards, obedient to the great law of spirit evolution, which is different from the evolution of matter. The latter is symbolical of, but does not explain, the process of the former. We are not individuals now, in our present earthly environment. We shall not have reached individuality until we shall have ascended to the higher state, when the divine spirit within us will have a perfect medium for the expression of its attributes.

Q. — What is your explanation of the problem presented to Christ, as to whether it was the infant itself or its parents that had sinned, that it was born blind?

A. — While the question of sin does not enter into the problem, I am convinced that the blindness was due to some act on the part of the spirit of the child in a previous incarnation. In my opinion such problems are only explicable on the hypothesis of a prior earthly existence.

Q. — Do our spirits pass at death into a state of happiness?

A. — Death is only a change of condition: time and space are in you, you are not in time and space. It is enough to know that as we make our lives purer and nobler, either in the seen or the unseen world, the nearer we approach God, who is the centre of all spiritual beauty and eternal joy.

Q. — What is the Hindu theory of the transmigration of souls?

A. — It is on the same basis as the theory of conservation is to the scientist. This theory was first produced by a philosopher of my country. The ancient sages did not believe in a creation. A creation implies producing something out of nothing. That is impossible. There was no beginning of creation as there was no beginning of time. God and creation are as two lines without end, without beginning, and parallel. Our theory of creation is "It is, it was, and is to be". All punishment is but reaction. People of the West should learn one thing from India and that is toleration. All the religions are good, since the essentials are the same.

Q. — Why are the women of India not much elevated?

A. — It is in a great degree owing to the barbarous invaders through different ages; it is partly due to the people of India themselves.

When it was pointed out to Swamiji in America that Hinduism is not a proselytising religion, he replied:

"I have a message to the West as Buddha had a message to the East."

Q. — Do you intend to introduce the practices and rituals of the Hindu religion into this country (America)?

A. — I am preaching simply philosophy.

Q. — Do you not think if the fear of future hell-fire were taken from man there would be no controlling him?

A. — No! On the contrary, I think he is made far better through love and hope than through fear.

Selections from the Math Diary

(Translated from Bengali)

Q. — Whom can we call a Guru?

A. — He who can tell your past and future is your Guru.

Q. — How can one have Bhakti?

A. — There is Bhakti within you, only a veil of lust-and-wealth covers it, and as soon as that is removed Bhakti will manifest by itself.

Q. — What is the true meaning of the assertion that we should depend on ourselves?

A. — Here self means the eternal Self. But even dependence on the non-eternal self may lead gradually to the right goal, as the individual self is really the eternal Self under delusion.

Q. — If unity is the only reality, how could duality which is perceived by all every moment have arisen?

A. — Perception is never dual; it is only the representation of perception that involves duality. If perception were dual, the known could have existed independently of the knower, and vice versa.

Q. — How is harmonious development of character to be best effected?

A. — By association with persons whose character has been so developed.

Q. — What should be our attitude to the Vedas?

A. — The Vedas, i.e. only those portions of them which agree with reason, are to be accepted as authority. Other Shâstras, such as the Purânas etc., are only to be accepted so far as they do not go against the Vedas. All the religious thoughts that have come subsequent to the Vedas, in the world, in whatever part of it have been derived from the Vedas.

Q. — Is the division of time into four Yugas astronomical or arbitrary calculation?

A. — There is no mention of such divisions in the Vedas. They are arbitrary assumptions of Paurânika times.

Q. — Is the relation between concepts and words necessary and immutable, or accidental and conventional?

A. — The point is exceedingly debatable. It seems that there is a necessary relation, but not absolutely so, as appears from the diversity of language. There may be some subtle relation which we are not yet able to detect.

Q. — What should be the principle to be followed in working within India? A.— First of all, men should be taught to be practical and physically strong. A dozen of such lions will conquer the world, and not millions of sheep can do so. Secondly, men should not be taught to imitate a personal ideal, however great.

Then Swamiji went on to speak of the corruptions of some of the Hindu symbols. He distinguished between the path of knowledge and the path of devotion. The former belonged properly to the Aryas, and therefore was so strict in the selection of Adhikâris (qualified aspirants), and the latter coming from the South, or non-Aryan sources, made no such distinction.

Q. — What part will the Ramakrishna Mission take in the

regenerating work of India?

A. — From this Math will go out men of character who will deluge the world with spirituality. This will be followed by revivals in other lines. Thus Brahmins, Kshatriyas, and Vaishyas will be produced. The Shudra caste will exist no longer — their work being done by machinery. The present want of India is the Kshatriya force.

Q. — Is retrograde reincarnation from the human stage possible?

A. — Yes. Reincarnation depends on Karma. If a man accumulates Karma akin to the beastly nature, he will be drawn thereto.

In one of the question-classes (1898) Swamiji traced image-worship to Buddhistic sources. First, there was the Chaitya; second, the Stupa ; and then came the temple of Buddha. Along with it arose the temples of the Hindu deities.

Q. — Does the Kundalini really exist in the physical body?

A. — Shri Ramakrishna used to say that the so-called lotuses of the Yogi do not really exist in the human body, but that they are created within oneself by Yoga powers.

Q. — Can a man attain Mukti by image-worship?

A. — Image-worship cannot directly give Mukti; it may be an indirect cause, a help on the way. Image-worship should not be condemned, for, with many, it prepares the mind for the realisation of the Advaita which alone makes man perfect.

Q. — What should be our highest ideal of character?

A. — Renunciation.

Q. — How did Buddhism leave the legacy of corruption in India?

A. — The Bauddhas tried to make everyone in India a monk or a nun. We cannot expect that from every one. This led to gradual relaxation among monks and nuns. It was also caused by their imitating Tibetan and other barbarous customs in the name of religion. They went, to preach in those places and assimilated their corruptions, and then introduced them into India.

Q. — Is Mâyâ without beginning and end?

A. — Maya is eternal both ways, taken universally, as genus; but it is non-eternal individually.

Q. — Brahman and Maya cannot be cognised simultaneously. How could the absolute reality of either be proved as arising out of the one or the other?

A. — It could be proved only by realisation. When one realises Brahman, for him Maya exists no longer, just as once the identity of the rope is found out, the illusion of the serpent comes no more.

Q. — What is Maya?

A. — There is only one thing, call it by any name — matter, or spirit. It is difficult or rather impossible to think the one independent of the other. This is Maya, or ignorance.

Q. — What is Mukti (liberation)?

A. — Mukti means entire freedom — freedom from the bondages of good and evil. A golden chain is as much a chain as an iron one. Shri Ramakrishna used to say that, to pick out one thorn which has stuck into the foot, another thorn is requisitioned, and when the thorn is taken out, both are thrown away. So the bad tendencies are to be counteracted by the good ones, but after that, the good tendencies have also to be conquered.

Q. — Can salvation (Mukti) be obtained without the grace of God?

A. — Salvation has nothing to do with God. Freedom already is.

Q. — What is the proof of the self in us not being the product of the body etc.?

A. — The "ego" like its correlative "non-ego", is the product of the body, mind etc. The only proof of the existence of the real Self is realisation.

Q. — Who is a true Jnâni, and who is a true Bhakta?

A. — The true Jnani is he who has the deepest love within his heart and at the same time is a practical seer of Advaita in his outward relations. And the true Bhakta (lover) is he who, realising his own soul as identified with the universal Soul, and thus possessed of the true Jnana within, feels for and loves everyone. Of Jnana and Bhakti he who advocates one and denounces the other cannot be either a Jnani or a Bhakta, but he is a thief and a cheat.

Q. — Why should a man serve Ishvara?

A. — If you once admit that there is such a thing as Ishvara (God), you have numberless occasions to serve Him. Service of the Lord means, according to all the scriptural authorities, remembrance (Smarana). If you believe in the existence of God, you will be reminded of Him at every step of your life.

Q. — Is Mâyâvâda different from Advaitâvada?

A. — No. They are identical. There is absolutely no other explanation of Advaitavada except Mayavada.

Q. — How is it possible for God who is infinite to be limited in the form of a man (as an Avatâra)?

A. — It is true that God is infinite, but not in the sense in which you comprehend it. You have confounded your idea of infinity with the materialistic idea of vastness. When you say that God cannot take the form of a man, you understand that a very, very large substance or form (as if material in nature), cannot be compressed into a very, very small compass. God's infinitude refers to the unlimitedness of a purely spiritual entity, and as such, does not suffer in the least by expressing itself in a human form.

Q. — Some say, "First of all become a Siddha (one who has realised the Truth), and then you have the right to Karma, or work for others", while others say that one should work for others even from the beginning. How can both these views be reconciled?

A. — You are confusing one thing with the other. Karma means either service to humanity or preaching. To real preaching, no doubt, none has the right except the Siddha Purusha, i.e. one who has realised the Truth. But to service every one has the right, and not only so, but every one is under obligation to serve others, so long as he is accepting service from others.

V. YOGA, VAIRAGYA, TAPASYA, LOVE

Q. — Does Yoga serve to keep the body in its full health and vitality?

A. — It does. It staves off disease. As objectification of one's own body is difficult, it is very effective in regard to others. Fruit and milk are the best food for Yogis.

Q. — Is the attainment of bliss synchronous with that of Vairagya?

A. — The first step in Vairagya is very painful. When perfected, it yields supreme bliss.

Q. — What is Tapasyâ?

A. — Tapasya is threefold — of the body, of speech and of mind. The first is service of others; the second truthfulness; and third, control and concentration.

Q. — Why do we not see that the same consciousness pervades the ant as well as the perfected sage?

A. — Realising the unity of this manifestation is a question of time only.

Q. — Is preaching possible without gaining perfection?

A. — No. May the Lord grant that all the Sannyasin disciples of my Master and of myself be perfected, so that they may be fit for missionary work!

Q. — Is the divine majesty expressed in the Universal Form of Shri Krishna in the Gita superior to the expression of love unattended with other attributes, embodied in the form of Shri Krishna, for instance, in His relation with the Gopis?

A. — The feeling of love, unattended with the idea of divinity, in respect to the person loved, is assuredly inferior to the expression of divine majesty. If it were not so, all lovers of the flesh would have obtained freedom.

VI. In Answer To Nivedita

(In answer to a few questions put by Sister Nivedita, Swamiji jotted down the replies on May 24 , 1900 at San Francisco.)

Q. — I cannot remember what parts Prithvi Rai and Chând disguised themselves to play, when they determined to attend the Svayamvara at Kanauj.

A. — Both went as minstrels.

Q. — Also did Prithvi Rai determine to marry Samyuktâ partly because she was the daughter of his rival and partly for the fame of her great beauty? Did he then send a woman-servant to obtain the post of her maid? And did this old nurse set herself to make the princess fall in love with Prithvi Rai?

A. — They had fallen in love with each other, hearing deeds and beauty and seeing portraits. Falling in love through portraits is an old Indian game.

Q. — How did Krishna come to be brought up amongst the shepherds?

A. — His father had to flee with the baby to save it from the tyrant Kamsa, who ordered all the babes (male) from that year to be killed, as (through prophecy) he was afraid one of them would be Krishna and dethrone him. He kept Krishna's father and mother in prison (who were his cousins) for fear of that prophecy.

Q. — How did this part of his life terminate?

A. — He came with his brother Baladeva and Nanda, his foster-father, invited by the tyrant to a festival. (The tyrant had plotted his destruction.) He killed the tyrant and instead of taking the throne placed the nearest heir on it. Himself he never took any fruit of action.

Q. — Can you give me any dramatic incident of this period?

A. — This period is full of miracles. He as a baby was once naughty and the cowherd-mother tried to tie him with her churning string and found she could not bind him with all the strings she had. Then her eyes opened and she saw that she was going to bind him who had the whole universe in his body. She began to pray and tremble. Immediately the Lord touched her with his Maya and she saw only the child.

Brahmâ, the chief of gods, disbelieving that the Lord had become a cowherd, stole one day all the cows and cowherd boys and put them to sleep in a cave. When he came back, he found the same boys and cows round Krishna. Again he stole the new lot and hid them away. He came back and saw there the same again. Then his eyes opened and began to see numerous worlds and heavens and Brahmans by the thousands, one greater than the preceding, in the body of the Lord.

He danced on the serpent Kâliya who had been poisoning the water of the Yamunâ, and he held up the mount Govardhana in defiance of Indra whose worship he had forbidden and who in revenge wanted to kill all the people of Vraja by deluge of rain. They were all sheltered by Krishna under the hill Govardhana which he upheld with a finger on their head.

He from his childhood was against snake-worship and Indra-worship. Indra-worship is a Vedic ritual. Throughout the Gita he is not favourable to Vedic ritual.

This is the period of his love to Gopis. He was eleven years of age.

VII. Guru, Avatara, Yoga, Japa, Seva

Q. — How can Vedanta be realised?

A. — By "hearing, reflection, and meditation". Hearing must take place from a Sad-guru. Even if one is not a regular disciple, but is a fit aspirant and hears the Sad-guru's words, he is liberated.

Q. — Who is a Sad-guru?

A. — A Sad-guru is one on whom the spiritual power has descended by Guru-paramparâ, or an unbroken chain of discipleship.

To play the role of a spiritual teacher is a very difficult thing. One has to take on oneself the sins of others. There is every chance of a fall in less advanced men. If merely physical pain ensues, then he should consider himself fortunate.

Q. — Cannot the spiritual teacher make the aspirant fit?

A. — An Avatâra can. Not an ordinary Guru.

Q. — Is there no easy way to liberation?

A. — "There is no royal road to Geometry" — except for those who have been fortunate enough to come in contact with an Avatara. Paramahamsa Deva used to say, "One who is having his last birth shall somehow or other see me."

Q. — Is not Yoga an easy path to that?

A. — (Jokingly) You have said well, I see! — Yoga an easy path! If your mind be not pure and you try to follow Yoga, you will perhaps attain some supernatural power, but that will be a hindrance. Therefore purity of mind is the first thing necessary.

Q. — How can this be attained?

A. — By good work. Good work is of two kinds, positive and negative. "Do not steal" — that is a negative mandate, and "Do good to others" — is a positive one.

Q. — Should not doing good to others be performed in a higher stage, for if performed in a lower stage, it may bind one to the world?

A. — It should be performed in the first stage. One who has any desire at first gets deluded and becomes bound, but not others. Gradually it will become very natural.

Q. — Sir, last night you said, "In you is everything." Now, if I want to be like Vishnu, shall I have to meditate on the form also, or only on the idea?

A. — According to capacity one may follow either way.

Q. — What is the means of realisation?

A. — The Guru is the means of realisation. "There is no knowledge without a teacher."

Q. — Some say that there is no necessity of practicing meditation in a worship-room. How far is it true?

A. — Those who have already realised the Lord's presence may not require it, but for others it is necessary. One, however, should go beyond the form and meditate on the impersonal aspect of God, for no form can grant liberation. You may get worldly prosperity from the sight of the form. One who ministers to his mother succeeds in this world; one who worships his father goes to heaven; but the worshipper of a Sâdhu (holy man) gets knowledge and devotion.

Q. — What is the meaning of " " etc. — Even a moment's association with the holy ones serves to take one beyond this relative existence"?

A. — A fit person coming in contact with a true Sadhu attains to liberation. True Sadhus are very rare, but their influence is such that a great writer has said, "Hypocrisy is the tribute which vice pays to virtue." But Avataras are Kapâlamochanas, that is, they can alter the doom of people. They can stir the whole world. The least dangerous and best form of worship is worshipping man. One who has got the idea of Brahman in a man has realised it in the whole universe. Monasticism and the householder's life are both good, according to different circumstances. Knowledge is the only thing necessary.

Q. — Where should one meditate — inside the body or outside it? Should the mind be withdrawn inside or held outside?

A. — We should try to meditate inside. As for the mind being here or there, it will take a long time before we reach the mental plane. Now our struggle is with the body. When one acquires a perfect steadiness in posture, then and then alone one begins to struggle with the mind. Âsana (posture) being conquered, one's limbs remain motionless, and one can sit as long as one pleases.

Q. — Sometimes one gets tired of Japa (repetition of the Mantra). Should one continue it or read some good book instead?

A. — One gets tired of Japa for two reasons. Sometimes one's brain is fatigued, sometimes it is the result of idleness. If the former, then one should give up Japa for the time being, for persistence in it at the time results in seeing hallucinations, or in lunacy etc. But if the latter, the mind should be forced to continue Japa.

Q. — Sometimes sitting at Japa one gets joy at first, but then one seems to be disinclined to continue the Japa owing to that joy. Should it be continued then?

A.— Yes, that joy is a hindrance to spiritual practice, its name being Rasâsvâdana (tasting of the sweetness). One must rise above that.

Q. — Is it good to practice Japa for a long time, though the mind may be wandering?

A. — Yes. As some people break a wild horse by always keeping his seat on his back.

Q. — You have written in your Bhakti-Yoga that if a weak-bodied man tries to practice Yoga, a tremendous reaction comes. Then what to do?

A. — What fear if you die in the attempt to realise the Self! Man is not afraid of dying for the sake of learning and many other things, and why should you fear to die for religion?

Q. — Can Jiva-sevâ (service to beings) alone give Mukti ?

A. — Jiva-seva can give Mukti not directly but indirectly, through the purification of the mind. But if you wish to do a thing properly, you must, for the time being, think that that is all-sufficient. The danger in any sect is want of zeal. There must be constancy (Nishthâ), or there will be no growth. At present it has become necessary to lay stress on Karma.

Q. — What should be our motive in work — compassion, or any other motive?

A. — Doing good to others out of compassion is good, but the Seva (service) of all beings in the spirit of the Lord is better.

Q. — What is the efficacy of prayer?

A. — By prayer one's subtle powers are easily roused, and if consciously done, all desires may be fulfilled by it; but done unconsciously, one perhaps in ten is fulfilled. Such prayer, however, is selfish and should therefore be discarded.

Q. — How to recognise God when He has assumed a human form?

A. — One who can alter the doom of people is the Lord. No Sadhu, however advanced, can claim this unique position. I do not see anyone who realises Ramakrishna as God. We sometimes feel it hazily, that is all. To realise Him as God and yet be attached to the world is inconsistent.

www.ingramcontent.com/pod-product-compliance
Lightning Source LLC
Chambersburg PA
CBHW050027170726
48282CB00025B/573

* 9 7 8 9 3 6 8 4 9 6 4 8 9 *